The Peace That You Seek

Messages of Guidance
for Souls
on the
Path of Awakening

Alan Cohen

Illustrations by
Michael Stillwater

THE PEACE THAT YOU SEEK
© 1985, 1991 by Alan Cohen

ISBN 0-910367-35-3

Cover art by Ki Vision. For information about the inspiring art of Ki, contact Ki Vision, 160 Seminary Drive, Suite 3B, Mill Valley, CA 94941.

Jacket design by Patt Narrowe

Illustrations by Michael Stillwater

To order *The Peace That You Seek:*

Personal Orders:
To order by Visa, MasterCard, or American Express, call:

1 (800) 462-3013
Monday-Friday 9AM-5PM Pacific Time
*Toll-free number for orders
and catalog requests only*

Or write:

Alan Cohen Publications
P. O. Box 95109
Des Moines, Washington 98198

For a free catalog of Alan Cohen's books, tapes, and workshop schedule, write or call the address or telephone number above.

Bookstore Orders:
The Peace That You Seek is available from these distributors of fine inspirational books:

Aquarian Book Dist.	Lotus Light
Baker & Taylor	Moving Books
Bookpeople	New Leaf Distributing Co.
De Vorss & Co.	Whole Health Book Co.

BY ALAN COHEN

Books
Companions of the Heart
Dare to Be Yourself
Have You Hugged a Monster Today?
The Healing of the Planet Earth
Joy Is My Compass
The Peace That You Seek
Rising in Love
Setting the Seen

Cassette Tapes
Deep Relaxation
                with music by Steven Halpern
Eden Morning
I Believe In You
                with songs & music by Stephen Longfellow Fiske
Miracle Mountain
Peace
                with music by Steven Halpern

Video
Dare To Be Yourself

To the Masters of the Great White Lodge,

whose guiding presence

uplifts souls of noble aspiration

and blesses the world.

The Peace That You Seek

The peace that you seek is found within yourself. This is the truth that you came to learn, and the only one that will satisfy you. For years and lifetimes have you sought after persons, objects, and experiences, in vain attempts to find the answer to your soul's longing; yet all of your travails have led only to disappointment in the things of the world.

Now, beloveds, now are you ready to accept the treasure of your heart's quest, found within your own soul. Here is where your search began, and here does it conclude, for love is completed only by itself.

The peace that you seek is found within yourself, and blessed are you who discover completion in the Home that has been prepared for you since time began, and where all seeking ends in the gentle arms of Spirit.

The Peace
That You Seek

The Remembrance of Divinity   1

The Way of the Light   29

The Guiding Spirit   51

There is Only Love   73

The Healing Presence   109

The Beams of Virtue   121

The Crest Jewels of Illumination   161

Fear Not in the Valley   181

The Golden Destiny   195

The Remembrance of Divinity

You Are The Light

There is a you
that has no beginning and no end,
a Divine Self
that lives above time, limitation,
and appearances.
To know your real self
you must lift your mind
into the reality that knows no
boundaries,
change, or fear.
This is the you
that your heart has longed to know,
the only you
that can bring you real peace.

Child of the Light,
Child of the Truth,
Child of the Word:
Your time has come
to rise above the quagmire of earth
and claim the destiny
for which you were created.

You were not made to wallow
in the pits of earthly limitation.
You were born to soar in the heavens
and touch the garment of the Christ.
You were made to claim the destiny
that has been held in trust for you
since you turned away
from your Heavenly Home.

You are destined for greater joy
than your mind has imagined.
Your lot is not suffering,
but greatness and majesty
befitting the Child of a King.
You will enter the Kingdom
that has awaited you
as you wandered on the earth.

Child of Light, come home now.
You have all but exhausted
the turns and byways
that attracted you
as you averted your eyes from the sun
toward the darkness.

Know that there is no loss,
death is not real,
and you have never truly been separate
from your Divine Source.
You are but one tiny thought from the
Estate that your heart has yearned for
in your years of scarcity.

Be deluded no longer
to believe that there is a fulfillment
outside the wonder that is you.
You are the fulfillment
you have sought.
You are the goal
you have longed to achieve.
Yours is the love
you have prayed to receive.
You are the way, the truth, and the life.

My Creed

There is but one creed I stand for:
the existence of God and none other.
There is but one belief I live for:
the reality of the Light
that outshines any image
that arises in form
and then passes away.
There is but one name that I have,
and that is Truth.
And there is but one soul that I live for,
and that is you.

If you believe in yourself
as a Child of the Light,
you know yourself as I know you.
If you accept yourself,
you stand with me
in my reverence for all of creation.
When you share my vision
you realize yourself to be one with me.

This is my first and final teaching.

The Lost Race

There is a lost race on the planet earth. It is a race of angelic beings seeded with the vision of the God who formed and blessed all things. Over the ages this race has been covered with a dust of delusional thoughts, misconceptions of self-identity, and erroneous concepts of the purpose of living. The race has not been in the least tainted, but it has forgotten its real nature.

This race is the Children of Light, and you are a part of it. You have fallen into the stupor of believing that you are a body, a configuration of emotions, and a self-contradicting intellect. Yet all of these are but disguises which cover the real you, hiding in the play of earth.

Know, now, the true purpose of all of your experience: Every breath, every action, every moment of your temporal existence brings you to the remembrance of your identity.   Seek not to superimpose false purposes and meaningless gods over the love that you are. The reality that you have come to express is peace.

Child of Light, acknowledge your perfection. Make a stand for the *real* purpose of your life; you are awakening to holiness.   With this single, simple thought you will gather all of your brethren into the fold of Heaven. The whole of humanity is knocking at the door of your heart with begging bowls of fear and misfortune, pleading to be told of the light that shines beyond their closed eyes. You have the power to nourish every soul that starves for the Truth. Acknowledge your own identity and admit every lost soul to the halls of Heaven.

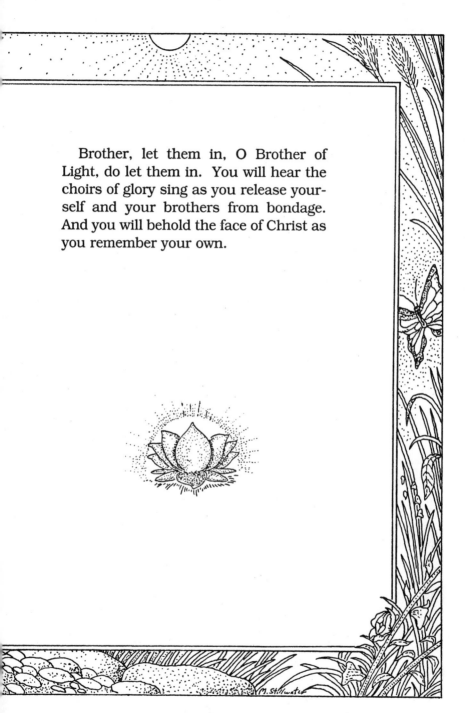

Brother, let them in, O Brother of Light, do let them in. You will hear the choirs of glory sing as you release yourself and your brothers from bondage. And you will behold the face of Christ as you remember your own.

Heartbeats

All life flows from spirit.
Your heart pulsates
from the center of the cosmos
and out to all creation.
You are a vehicle for God's love
to bless the world.
Your Heavenly Father needs your love
to complete His purpose for creation,
which is the same as yours.

Come and acknowledge
the miracle of your loving being;
it is time for you to know
the source of all good.
You are a beat in the heart of God.
All of life is blessed through you.

The Dawn of God

Only faulty thinking
has created death and disease,
poverty of spirit,
and all sense of loss.

The time of misunderstanding
is now come to an end.
Truth must have its way.
Your suffering must cease,
and your divinity be manifested.

This is the gateway to the Kingdom
that you have journeyed so far to find.

This is the moment of the dawn,
the vision of the Light
that has no beginning or end.

The time of God is at hand,
and so is the majesty of your soul.
Stand tall and firm
in the knowledge that you are blessed.

The Message of Love

This is the Message of Love from the eternal to the finite, from the formless to the form, from the Father to the Child. Here is the doorway to your freedom, the entrance to your home.

Choose now the healing of your own soul. In your enlightenment is the removal of all suffering, an offering of love that is completely shared. There is no selfishness in your own realization. To deny your identity would be to withhold Heaven from those who need it and postpone the consummation of human evolution from all who have given so painfully to find it.

There is but one soul: the Soul of God. You are a ray of love emanating brightly from the Sun that is our Source.

The Gift You Were Born To Share

Give, now, the gift you were born to share: the celebration of your oneness with perfect beauty. You are free to reveal your loving nature to all of the universe and allow all living things to share in the blessing that is you.

Child of the Stars, step forth and shine!

Child of Wonder, express the nobility in which you were created. Stir the hearts of your brethren to remember their ancient heritage, hidden but never lost.

Child of God, be divine. You were born to know yourself as a perfect expression of Christ.

Child of Love, be who you are!

One God

Now must end the division of God into parts. You have robbed yourself of divinity by seeing separation where there is unity.

How difficult life becomes when you deny your own light! You have taken Truth and twisted it to reflect darkness. You have taken inspiration and cast it aside in deference to archaic forms. You have borne witness to the Christ and falsified your vision to uphold a self-image created in hell. Children of Light, Knights of the Highest Nobility, Masters of Compassion, come forth into the celebration of your real identity.

Speak no more of abandonment and woe, but lift up your weeping eyes and behold the countenance of the Living

God, standing before you with the gift of complete forgiveness.

Your foolish unworthiness has bent you in shame, but you are of the Highest of the High, born in the majesty of the Creator, the seed of the stars.

Wait no more for the acknowledgement of your glory. The ages are bloodied with false ambitions and hopeless hopes. The history of the world is a record of foolishness; its pain calls out to angels at the farthest star.

Peace is your right. Tarry not. Doubt not. Fear not. All such procrastinations are the waverings of fools. The One God is a God of Love, and only love, of peace, and of harmony.

Remember unity, and you remember yourself.

How Perfect the Way

You need only one lesson,
for you have made but one mistake:
an error in *consciousness,*
in mind —
but never in truth.

You are as new as the moment
you were shined into life
from the heart of God.
Your radiant Self
has not been touched or tainted
by earthly experience
or any darkness you have perceived.
Your errors have been
in perception alone,
and thus your return is accomplished
by correction in thought alone.

How simple is salvation!
How easy the fulfillment of your destiny!
How perfect the way to completion!

Your Purity

Your purity is eternal.
No force could ever intrude
upon the love that is you.
There *is* no force outside of the love
that is you.
Your purity shines
like a beacon in a dark night.
Let no mortal thoughts
stand between you
and the truth of your being.
You *are* the truth of your being.

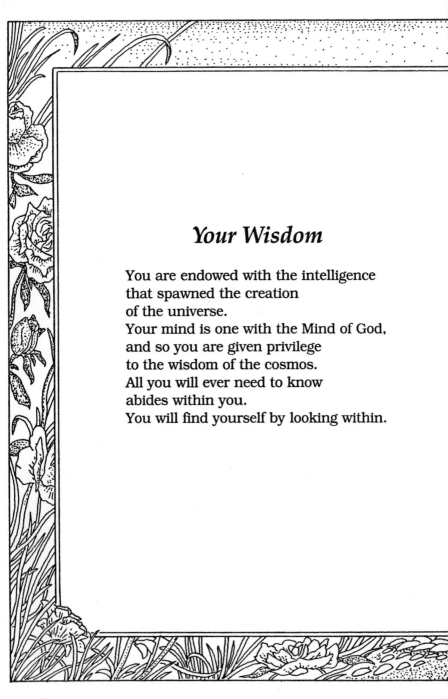

Your Wisdom

You are endowed with the intelligence
that spawned the creation
of the universe.
Your mind is one with the Mind of God,
and so you are given privilege
to the wisdom of the cosmos.
All you will ever need to know
abides within you.
You will find yourself by looking within.

Your Power

Your power is the power of all the universe.

Your radiance is that of the sun, the stars, and every comet that lights the heavens.

Your strength is brimming in every atom of creation, every flash of insight, every explosion of genius streaming through the breast of the inspired artist.

Your energy is forged into the miracles you work like a beacon signaling the end of a long and bitter night.

Your commitment is the might of all the universe. Your power was given you to uplift every life you touch, and leave the world blazing with the fire of the Holy Spirit.

Your power is the power of God.

M. Stillwater

You Are a Force

You are not a person or a thing,
but a *force.*

You are a dynamo of good
that God has breathed into life
to infuse truth into the earth plane.

Every moment
you are creating a new world,
a new lifestream
from which greater lives
will grow and develop.

You must act in accord
with the responsibility for greatness.

Blessings

You are completely blessed.

Your soul is as dear to God
as that of Jesus,
Moses,
Buddha,
Mohammed,
and every angel
in the whole of the universe.

There is no sin that you could commit
that could cause you
to lose the blessing of God.
Sin, evil, and damnation
are dark dreams of the mortal mind,
entirely unknown
to the Holy Spirit within you,
which shines forever.
Your life shines
with the light of your Creator.

The Initiation

The masters are calling you to initiation.
Your moment has come
to claim the scepter of life
that sparkles with
the blessing of the divine.
You are called to step
into the hall of wisdom
and accept the charge
of the Son of God.

Your fears and doubts may assail you
in a last attempt to return you
to a world
which has yielded only rancid fruit.
Old identities may beckon you
to their attention,
though substance they have not.

Beliefs in darkness may tempt you
to turn from the knowledge
of the One Light.

Now you must adhere
to the bulwarks
of your memory of God,
firmly implanted in your bosom,
untouchable by murmurings of doubt.
Now you must stand firm
in the face of sterile thoughts.
Now you must declare perfection
before the appearance of error.
Now you must firmly declare,
"I am a Son of God."

Your task is clear,
and your goal the most worthy.
You are called to the initiation
of the Son of God.

The Christ In You

The Christ calls to you
to share His Light with you.
He reaches out in a summon
for the saviors of the world,
all who would invoke the power of love
to heal the planet
and all who share life with it.
His hand is extended to you,
gently inviting you to join
the force of men and women
who would bear witness
to the truth of untarnishable life.
The Christ is looking for healers.
Would you be one of them?

If so, simply acknowledge
the presence of God within you,
and you will find the endless blessings
that bring the peace of God
to the family of light
of which you are born.

The Messenger

You are the messenger
that God has chosen
to deliver good tidings
to weary soldiers on the battlefield.
You carry the cup of cooling water
to the parched lips
of a sore and tired humanity.
Your hands will cleanse
the lepers of disease
and restore dignity to the lame.

Accept your charge,
and complete the happy purpose
for which you entered life.

The Unwavering

There is one within you who is
    unwavering,
        steady of mind,
            and wholly pure of heart.

Let not your mind be disturbed,
    and your reality
        as the unwavering one
           will be established.

The Chosen People

The chosen people are those
who realize
that God has chosen them
as His beloveds,
who have chosen Him as their own,
and who know
that salvation will come to them
as they are willing to accept it.

The Way of
The Light

God Is the Path

There is no path.
There is only God.

Divine Forgetfulness

Forget everything
except your divine origin.
Nothing has happened,
but God.

The Source

There is one Source of all.
Know the Source,
and you will bless the fruit.

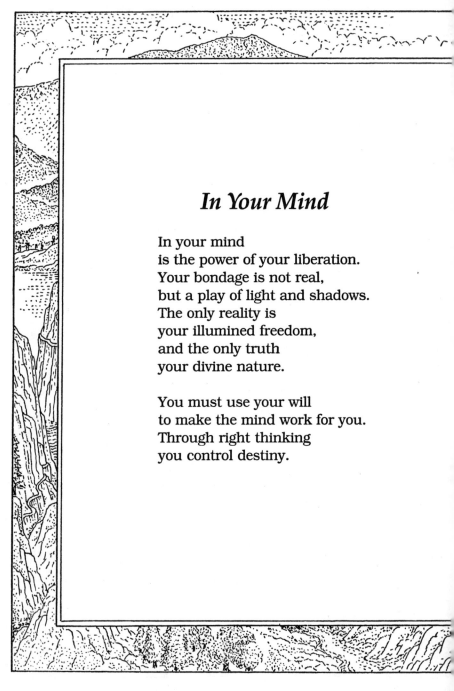

In Your Mind

In your mind
is the power of your liberation.
Your bondage is not real,
but a play of light and shadows.
The only reality is
your illumined freedom,
and the only truth
your divine nature.

You must use your will
to make the mind work for you.
Through right thinking
you control destiny.

What I Do With God

What I do with God must succeed. All the power of the universe is given unto me as I think, speak, and act with the One whose plan I have come to fulfill.

Everywhere I go, He makes the way clear for me. Everyone I meet, He unites with me. All the love I give, He returns in measure beyond measure. I know that His Love and mine are one.

I celebrate the perfection of all life! No effort or struggle is required of me, for His Life is joined with mine. His Word cannot fail. His Strength must overcome all appearances of opposition. His Light must shine peace into every situation where it is invited.

There is no God but God. There is no love but God's love. There is no plan but God's plan for the healing of all humanity. Everyone for whom I pray in His name must be healed. Everyone to whom I offer a smile of comfort must be relieved of their burden. Every star I see, the light of which awakens my thanks for His majesty, sparkles more brightly in the early morning sky.

Father, Your Will is finally mine, and for this I am grateful. No more would I attempt to impose a will other than Yours, and neither would I seek to accomplish goals that serve only themselves. Your Goal is now mine, and the reward of all life comes to me. You are my Father and I am your Son. You are the Source and I am one with You.

I celebrate the healing of Your Son. I acknowledge Your Light as mine and I accept the strength You have given me to use on Your behalf. My life is free of strife. Who could act on behalf of his Creator and experience conflict? Who could breathe the oneness of all that lives and know fear? Who could love with the Heart that knows no evil, and be alone in his world?

Father, I am finally one with You, only to realize that so have I been through all the ages. Dear Father, let me never leave You again. I will sing the song of Your glory to all of the world, sharing the good news that You are always with me, and that our time of separate thoughts is come to an end.

I am ready to take my place among the saviors of the world. I am a Child of the One who has promised to bring a peace beyond understanding to hearts that have nearly forgotten their origin. Father, I embrace You and I love You, and I pledge every breath unto Your glory. You are the One who has given me the life I love.

Providence

Your entire life is enfolded in providence. Your every step is softened in the golden sand that sparkles with the kiss of His Ocean. The infinite compassion of your Heavenly Father has washed away your errors with waves of forgiveness that leave the shore of your heart glistening and smooth.

Fear not. Your Beloved surrounds you with perfect peace until the end, which is really a beginning. You left your divine birthright in search of nothing, and that is what you have found. Now you are ready to come home.

Welcome, beloved one. God is your only strength.

The Comforter

The belief in abandonment

is the folly of life,

and constant providence

the great comforter.

Real Peace

The only real peace
is spiritual peace.
What men call peace
is but an interval between war.
The end of all strife comes
as you find God
within your own heart.

Your Ministry

Your ministry is where you are.
You do not need a steeple,
a congregation,
or a title.
You need only God,
and He is with you wherever you go.

Preach to the trees!
Extol His graces
to the surf of the sea!
Meditate in the silence of the dawn!
The church is within you,
and there I dwell with you always.

The Task At Hand

The clearest way to the light
is through the task at hand.
Acknowledge what is before you now,
love it,
and do what is required
to bring peace,
strength,
and healing.

You will be astonished
at the quickness
with which you find yourself
home.

Forms

There are many forms
through which your Heavenly Father
reveals Himself.
Your brethren travel pathways
that you follow not,
and yet they save you
the time and effort
of walking their way.
Honor your brothers' work,
for you are united with them
in purpose.
Thus you are free
to walk your way in confidence.

Renunciation

Renunciation is not sacrifice.

Love God,
and that which
does not serve you
will drop away from you
without your least effort.

The oak tree in summer
would work foolishly
to rid itself of the leaves
which gather its light.

In autumn
the gentlest of breezes
lifts away that which has
fulfilled its purpose.

Renunciation with struggle
is a folly of ego.

Good and Truth

Nothing is too good to be true.

Everything that is good is true.

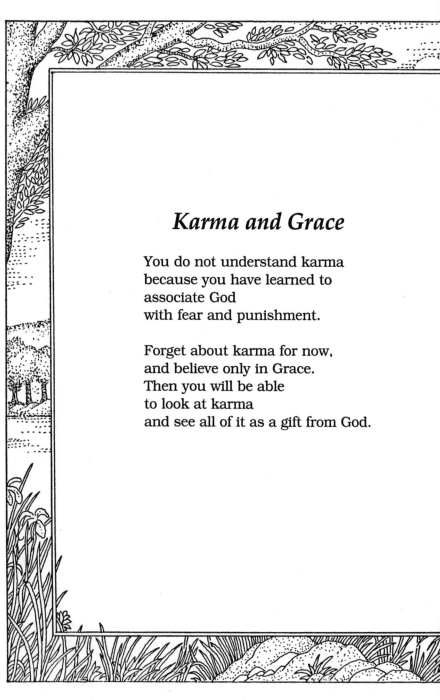

Karma and Grace

You do not understand karma
because you have learned to
associate God
with fear and punishment.

Forget about karma for now,
and believe only in Grace.
Then you will be able
to look at karma
and see all of it as a gift from God.

The Moment
of Forgiveness

Your errors are forgiven
the moment
you become aware of them.

The Evangelist

The only evangelist

is the truth.

What Is Important

The problem is not in choosing
between the alternatives.
You cannot choose
between alternatives,
for you have forgotten
what the alternatives are.

There is but one choice to make:
Peace or fear.
All else is illusion.
Let His Love be important,
and all choices
will make themselves for you.

The Guiding Spirit

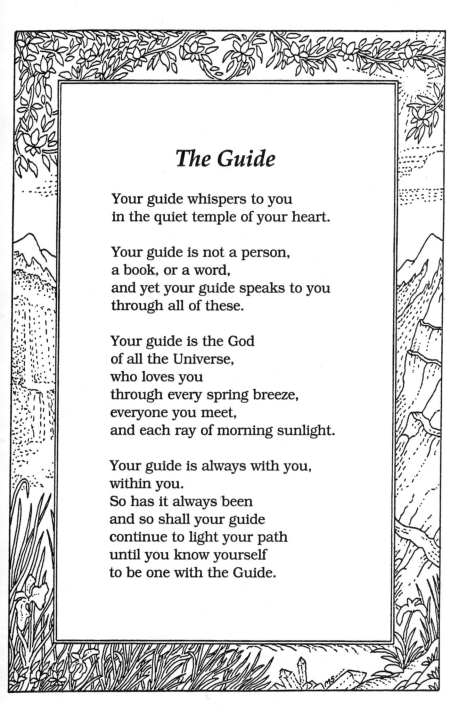

The Guide

Your guide whispers to you
in the quiet temple of your heart.

Your guide is not a person,
a book, or a word,
and yet your guide speaks to you
through all of these.

Your guide is the God
of all the Universe,
who loves you
through every spring breeze,
everyone you meet,
and each ray of morning sunlight.

Your guide is always with you,
within you.
So has it always been
and so shall your guide
continue to light your path
until you know yourself
to be one with the Guide.

The Master
Lives Within You

The master that you have sought in the outer world lives within your being. The blueprint for all creation is in your heart. The answer to all of your questions is contained in your own soul.

Seek no more for answers outside yourself. *You* are the answer. All of the teachers, guides, and gurus that you have worshipped outside yourself are but reflections of the divinity that you have denied as your own.

Now you must claim your identity as a master and live it to teach all that holiness resides within one's own nature.

Messages of Guidance

These messages are written by yourself, in words you understand because they belong to you. These thoughts speak from the center of your being, where the knowledge of your perfection has been held in trust for your awakening. The truth delights your spirit, while the false leaves no impression.

Do these words and those like them excite your heart and bring a thrill of hope to a grey and tired world? Do they stir within you a memory of the beauty and wonder that life can offer? Do they resonate in your soul and remind you that the fullness of the universe lies within you, where you are whole?

If so, you have discovered the Truth. The message of guidance has directed you to your own self. The guide has shown you the way to the bridge where the world touches Heaven.

The Pilot

There is a Pilot
to whom you can turn
in moments of confusion.
This unfailing wisdom
gently directs your way
to the way of the peaceful.

As you become more familiar
and comfortable
with the quiet feeling
that guides you
in moments of turmoil,
you will recognize
the simple song
of a happy heart.

The Loyal Friend

Your sense of Truth is infallible.

There is a mind in you that knows the truth of every situation and the way to overcome every challenge.

Do not seek to solve situations on the level of the reasoning mind, but seek within yourself to find the Divine Mind that knows the answer. This servant will help you resolve all difficulties, meet all needs, and rise above all thoughts of limitation.

The Truth is a loyal friend that travels with you wherever you go. Call upon it and it will serve you well.

Your True Nature

Your mission as a savior of the world is not accomplished through judgment or condemnation, but through living in peace.

You have claimed all the wrong attributes as your self: sin, sickness, lack, and limitation – all of the ideas that are foreign to your true nature. Yet it is these dreams that you have accepted as your identity, while you have denied all of the holy graces that you embody.

Children, the world you have made is the perfect opposite of the world into which you were born, and to which you are destined. Now you must accomplish a perfect reversal of thinking to find the answers to the questions you never had.

This transformation of thinking is not as arduous as you have thought, for truth is never as cumbersome as the maintenance of a belief system based on lies. To discover the truth you need only acknowledge that your source is within you, ever present, and eternally available. This is the easiest shift in all of your life, and really the only one you need make.

Your divinity is not a feat to be mastered; it is a reality to be accepted. This reality does not depend on your acceptance of it, but your appreciation of it does.

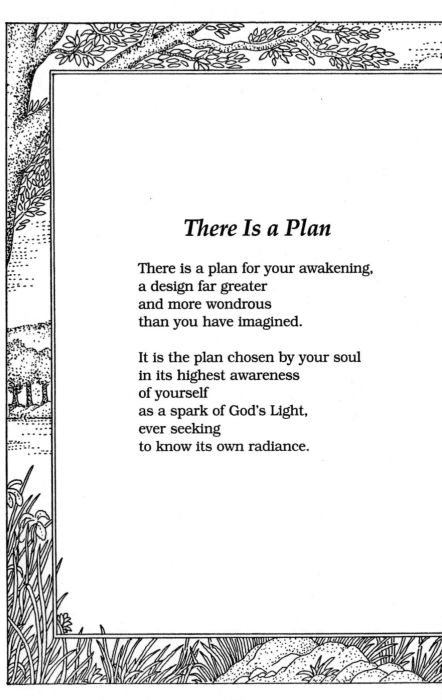

There Is a Plan

There is a plan for your awakening,
a design far greater
and more wondrous
than you have imagined.

It is the plan chosen by your soul
in its highest awareness
of yourself
as a spark of God's Light,
ever seeking
to know its own radiance.

Self-Understanding

The time of outer masters
is come to an end.
The age of self-understanding
is at hand.
This is accomplished
the moment you realize
that God lives within you
and radiates as you.

There is no separation
between you and the truth.
There is an infinitely untraversable
gap between who you are
and who you made yourself to be.

Your false identity
has no power over you
unless you attempt
to find refuge in it.
The only refuge is in Truth.

Be The Master

The time has passed for you
to seek the Master.
Now it is for you
to *be* the Master.
You live in a world
where the folly of seeking
has been substituted
for the fullness of knowing.

Always remember that you are
the Child of the Master
of a Great Estate,
and that in serving your Father
the fullness of His blessing
is yours.

Be the master now.

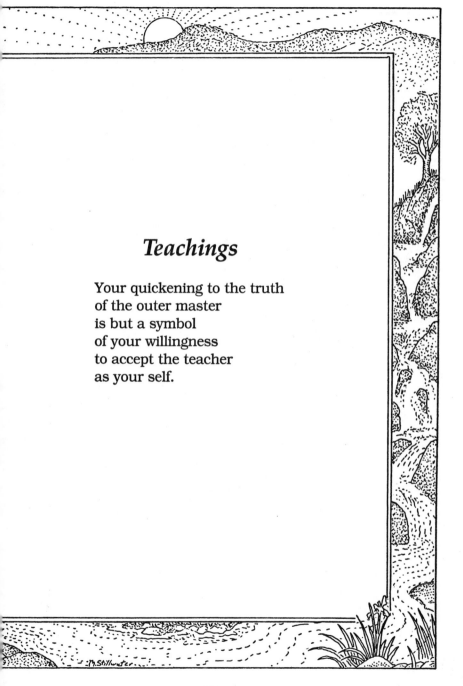

Teachings

Your quickening to the truth
of the outer master
is but a symbol
of your willingness
to accept the teacher
as your self.

Way-Showers

As you behold those who have found God, you will find that He is speaking to you through them.

Then He will speak through you to others.

Your peaceful actions are His words.

False Teachers

Do not blame false teachers
for your willingness to be misled.
Instead,
rejoice that you have learned
to follow Truth,
and not a person.

Your false teacher is your mirror.
You wanted a human savior,
and God freed you
from your willingness
to limit God to a body.

The only false teacher
is the thought that guides you
to a truth outside yourself.
The only real teacher
is the glory within you.

The Truth Is Whole

Do not settle for any truth less than the one which makes you whole. In your quest for God you have accepted half-hearted truths, partial blessings, and pretentious gurus. Your search was sincere, but your discrimination unkeen.

You have a right to a truth that fulfills you so completely that you need never again turn outward for blessings. Your authority as a Son or Daughter of the Universe entitles you to be wholly satisfied in body, mind, and spirit.

We urge you – nay, implore you – to accept only the teaching which fulfills the longing of your soul, for only when the soul is content does joy spring forth.

The truth is distinguishable by the consistent peace it brings to those who love it and are willing to walk its way in dignity.

Open Yourself

Always assume
that God is working for you.
Be open to all possibilities.

Know that God has new
and wonderful ideas for you,
and He will reveal more to you
each beautiful day.

Allow God to be your guide,
and miracles will open
all the doors of life.

Follow the Light

Follow the light. It will always help you. The light is God's gift of certain confidence in yourself when all the world seems to have deserted you. It is your friend in a time of need and your comforter in a time of sorrow. The light is the sign of God's love for His Children who have chosen to travel the far country.

Never believe that God could leave you. This is the only condition in all the universe that is impossible. God's caring for you is the truth that redeems you from all travail. When you feel your world disintegrating, turn to God. He will be there waiting for you, loving you eternally.

While you are following the Light that is God, God is following the Light that is you.

The Only Real Value

The Light is your only friend.

Because it is eternal,
it will never fail you.
Because it is real,
you can never lose it.
Because it goes with you
wherever you are,
you can never be in darkness.

The Light lives in you,
as you.

The Savior

The savior lives within your heart.
When you realize where He is,
you are saved.

There is Only Love

There Is Only Love

Love is the shining glory of all creation. Every being that has ever lived, every soul that has ever breathed, every heart that has ever beat, has been only for the sake of love. Be not deceived by appearances, for love is the light that shines beyond every dark thought or fearful dream. Children of the Highest Light, there is but one truth, the remembrance of which shall take you all the way home to your Father's Heavenly Kingdom: *There is only love.*

All of your fears, travails, and uncertainties fall away as nothing in the light of the benevolence that oversees you, holds you dear in its eternal arms, and blesses you with the kiss of dawn. Though you remember it not, you are paramountly dear to your Heavenly

Father. O divine one, let now be the happy moment of your remembrance. All of your past melts into the light as you offer all to Him who can heal it. Awake to the glory that abides within you! Acknowledge your true nature as a perfect Child of Light! And thank the Father with me, for there is only thanks to be given.

Sing the song of your redemption with the chorus of souls in accord that has traveled with you to the portals of eternity, invisible to your physical eyes, yet perfectly present and speedily attendant to your soul's calling. This is your day of release! This is the day of your salvation from fearful nightmares of limitation and fictitious fantasies of sin. This is the moment for which you have lived, strived, and breathed. This is your homecoming. The myriads of Heaven celebrate it with you, for your life has had no purpose but this one.

Wander no more in the labyrinths of confusion, but look up! Look up and see the reception that has awaited your glad acceptance since time began. This is the moment you have chosen for your release, and it is shared by all who have ever laughed in the light of the morning. And with your healing does all creation breathe easier, for your release is the end of all that never was, and the beginning of all that has always been.

The Divine Romance

Your relationships are your most fruitful opportunities for spiritual advancement. Embrace each moment of sharing with thanksgiving, for in every challenging relationship lies the key to your growth in spirit.

Use relationships as a way to let go of all that binds you to your sense of smallness. In truth you have no limitations at all, and your interactions with your brothers and sisters allow you to see what boundaries you believe you have. Let go of all of them! Release yourself from the bondage that you have carried for lifetimes! Be free of every idea of lack that has tied your mind to pain!

Go forth into a new life and see who you truly are. Your greatness shines brighter than the sun. Let it shine! Your divinity is that of the Christ. Let it be known! Your love is the heart of the entire universe! Let it flow!

You have a relationship with God, a divine union knowable through every breath, every rainbow, and every bright new morning. Let God be your lover and celebrate the Divine Romance.

Love Yourself

Love yourself
no matter what you do.

You are the gift
that God has given to the world.
He will never give up on you.
God has as much faith in you
as He has in Himself.

His love for you is not dependent
on anything you do,
any thought you think,
or any experience
through which you pass.
God's love is always a Cause,
and never an effect.
He knows who you are,
and His gratefulness for you
is eternally, perfectly ensured.

Your Real Relationship

Your relationship with God
is the only one
that can bring you real peace.

You can love God
through an earthly beloved,
but always remember
that the source of your love
is so much greater than a person.
The source of your love
is the Spirit
that fills the entire cosmos with song
and rejoices in your every heartbeat.

Let God be your true beloved
and you will find union everywhere.

Make Peace
With Your Parents

Your denial of your appreciation for your parents is the greatest error of your generation. You must realize the enormity of the spiritual power that is locked beyond your unwillingness to resolve your relationship with your parents. This is the key to the healing of *all* of your relationships.

All of these messages are given for the healing of your relationship with your parents. Search your heart and you will realize the deep love that you have for your earthly parents, and the incredible pain that you have created by denying your true affection for them. All of your resentments, resistances, and the isolating of yourself are but masks for the genuine love that you feel for them, the appreciation you fear to express.

Children, go home and make peace with your parents. They await your love like starving lepers longing for the touch of the Christ. Do not deny them the truth of your caring any longer. Share your love for them, completely, fully, and unashamedly. All disease will disappear before your eyes in a miracle that will astonish you with the swiftness of your own transformation.

Your parents committed no mistake against you that cannot be instantly healed by your forgiveness. The scars which you have seemingly inflicted upon them will disappear like the snow that melts on the first day of spring and heals the earth with its own release.

Children, do not seek any further on the spiritual path until you have made your parents your friends. No guru, book, diet, or meditation practice can do more for you than you can do for yourself by telling your parents of your great and sincere love for them. Save yourself much hardship, loneliness, and pain. Go home and embrace your mother and father. Look into their eyes and show them that your years of separation mean nothing now. Show them that their purpose in this life has been fulfilled. Do now the work of the Christ.

Hear my words, hear them well, and mark them: You may not call yourself my disciple if you bear antagonism or enmity toward your parents. My disciples bear only undying love for their earthly parents, for they understand that their parents are Myself in a form which has gone unrecognized. Those who encourage you to break the umbilicus of caring between you and your father and mother speak the word of dark and tearful separation that has brought great despair to your world. Listen within your heart and you will hear the melody of love sung by your real voice, joined with mine.

Weep not if your parents are no longer in the plane of earthly life. They are as real and alive and close to you as your desire to make peace with them; therefore speak to them in your heart and they will surely feel the ray of forgiveness which spans the worlds. The radiance of your healing love will touch the dead and restore them to spiritual life with one single thought of true caring. What has passed in flesh is yet reborn in spirit.

Try my word, Children, and prove it: Make peace with your parents. In so rising you will understand the whole of my life and my teaching. And this I promise you, with the certainty of the Word that I have taught: As you go to make peace with your parents, I shall surely walk with you.

And I guarantee to accomplish what you cannot. All blessings be with you in this, the holiest quest in which you shall most certainly succeed.

Perfect Accord

It was you who created
the Laws of Love,
and blessed are you
for having done so
with the touch of perfection
that signifies
your loving co-creatorship
with your Heavenly Father.

Behold,
a Father and Son
in perfect accord
create a reality
that yields only peace.

The Forgiving Light

You are forgiven.

See yourself in the forgiven light
in which your Heavenly Father
recognizes you,
and you have the key
to the healing of the world.

Friendship

All of the divine promises of God
may be experienced
through human friendship.
Because you can understand God
in human terms,
He is willing to reveal Himself
in your human affairs.

Seek to be all to your friends
that you would have God be to you,
and salvation's peace
will come to rest
in the temple of your heart.

God is your best,
most precious,
and only friend.

Brotherly Love

There is no difference
between Godly love
and brotherly love.

When you love your brother as God,
you will discover
that your brother *is* God.

*How To Bless
Your Brother*

The most powerful way
to bless your brother
is to see him as blessed.

You do not realize
the disservice you do him
and yourself
when you think of him
as less than whole.

Bless your brothers
by seeing their perfection,
and you will discover yourself
to be created in their holiness.

Your Brother's Request

Your brother wants
nothing from you
but love,

and there is nothing else
you want to
or possibly could
give him.

Your Brother's Happiness

When you find no purpose
in your own pain,
you will only rejoice
in your brother's happiness.
You cannot accept his freedom
until you accept your own.

When you see that all joy is shared,
you will want nothing but good
for everyone.

Reconciliation

When two estranged brothers

resolve their separation,

a ray of light is released

which shines the world

closer to Heaven.

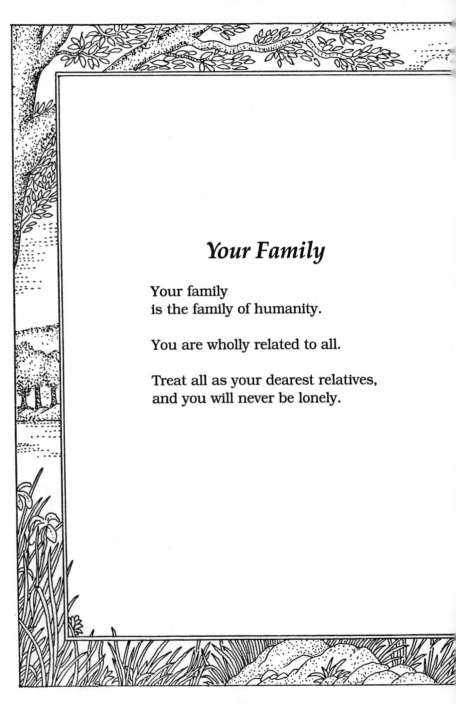

Your Family

Your family
is the family of humanity.

You are wholly related to all.

Treat all as your dearest relatives,
and you will never be lonely.

The Destiny of
All Relationships

Relationships do not end
because your relationship with God
could never end.

The destiny of all relationships
is to be transformed into perfect love.

If your relationship
seems to have ended in darkness,
do not be fooled by appearances,
but remember the truth of love.

Despair not,
for your relationship is not ended;
it will not be complete
until only the purest love
has replaced all fear,
and both of your hearts are content.

This is God's promise.

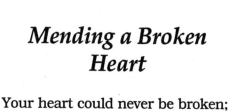

Mending a Broken Heart

Your heart could never be broken;
only the ego could be broken.
The idea that love could be divided
is an empty dream
that flees with the dawn.

Your heart is the Heart of Christ,
and that Heart
could no more be broken
than the light
could contain darkness.

Remember whose Heart is yours,
and you will recognize yourself
to be eternally whole
and filled with joy.

Marriage

Marriage is not an act you undertake, but an acknowledgement of what you already are. Do not confuse the touching of bodies with the unity of spirit. What God hath joined, no man could possibly put asunder.

True joining is a state of mind that runs far deeper than physical proximity. Bodies are a way to communicate the love that shines from your soul, but that love goes far beyond your physical form, and is indeed quite independent of it. Remember the love, and the bodies will be well cared for.

As you realize your true union in spirit, you will understand the real beauty of your relationship.

Children

Children are your teachers because they show you yourself. Your children bear you a double blessing: They mirror to you your own self-image as they bring you the refreshment of their innocent perception. Accept the gifts your children bring you. While you aid them in learning the lessons of this world, they teach you the lessons of the Kingdom.

Children are not blank slates upon which is written the training given them by their parents; that is only a small part of the picture. Your children are wise souls who have lessons to learn, and they have chosen you to help them to accomplish them in this lifetime.

Your children are with you by design. Your awareness of the perfection of your relationship with them will aid you deeply in gaining the lessons that your Father brings to you through your walking the path together.

Never see your children as inferior or subservient, but as equals in spirit. Speak to them as you would a whole person of strong spirit, and they will return your blessing. Physical age means nothing. The difference in your ages is unknown to God. Let go of your ideas of years and see your children and yourself in a new and wondrous light.

Support your children as they learn their lessons, but then you must release them as Children of the Universe. Trust

that your Heavenly Father is the same as theirs. He will care for them in the ways that you cannot. When you feel at a loss, that you can do no more for them than you have been doing, that is the time to entrust their well being and yours to the Holy Spirit, who will guide you perfectly, quietly, and gently to the peace you seek for yourself and your children.

The remembrance of your true identity is the key to helping your children remember theirs. We are all His Children.

No Measure

There is no measure
to the extent of my love for you.

All of your words,
concepts,
or understandings
are but reflections
of the preciousness
with which I adore you.

The only way
that you can begin to know
how much I love you
is to love your brethren.
Then you will know me
and yourself
fully.

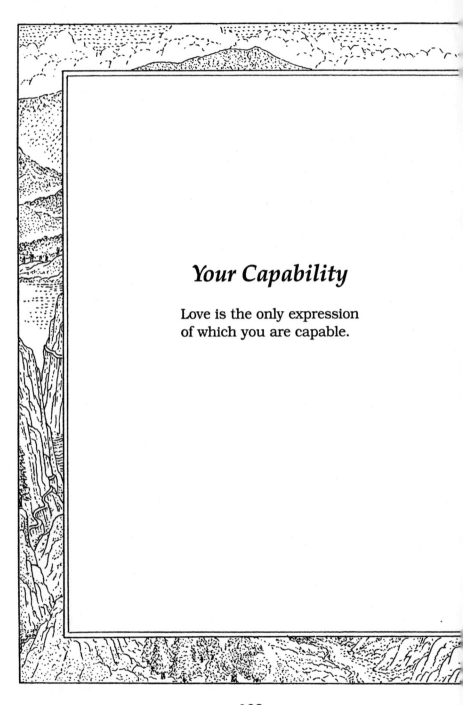

Your Capability

Love is the only expression
of which you are capable.

The Call For Love

The call for love
  is the hidden plea
    in every question,

      and giving love
        the only answer.

The Answer

The answer is Love.

What Love Can Solve

As you live in the light of love
    you see your path
        from the highest perspective,

and your course of action
    is made clear to you.

There is no problem in the universe
    that love cannot solve completely.

Real Conversion

You will win more for God by acknowledging perfection than by attempting to change another.

You serve your brother best by acknowledging his divinity. Let go of your attempt to save him. He will be helped more by your love than by judgment.

This is the only lesson that I taught, and the one that has been the most misused. Convert your brother with love, and you will win a great victory for the Kingdom, which is within you.

I love you unconditionally, and therefore the only gift I ask you to offer your brother is grace.

God has no consciousness of sin. Join me in the consciousness of purity, and the bells of forgiveness will signal the end of suffering throughout the world. Awaken with me to the holiness of all your brothers, and together we form a force of caring that cannot be resisted. Arise with me to the calling of the heart, the denial of which has caused the world to be so weary through needless attack upon shadows. Approach your brothers with complete love and you will find the peace that you lost in separating yourself from them. Thus you will find forgiveness for yourself.

You cannot live in a house divided against itself, and your house is yourself. The true family of humanity is united in the pure love of God. You help me most by loving your family just as it is. You will see miracles far greater than you imagined possible. Your life will be transformed into a holy offering fit for the altar of God, the only destiny you deserve.

My love is ever with you.

Everything and Nothing

If you have everything but love,
you have nothing.

If you have nothing but love,
you have everything.

The Healing
Presence

The Purpose of Healing

The purpose of all healing
is to reunite a soul
with its identity as Godly Light.

When you perform healing work,
seek not only to heal
the physical body,
but seek to know
and glorify
the perfect presence of God.

When the soul is healed,
all is seen and known as it is,
in pure perfection.

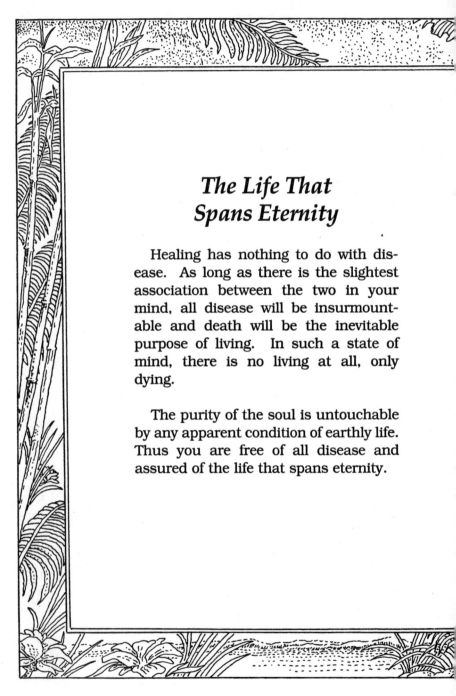

The Life That Spans Eternity

Healing has nothing to do with disease. As long as there is the slightest association between the two in your mind, all disease will be insurmountable and death will be the inevitable purpose of living. In such a state of mind, there is no living at all, only dying.

The purity of the soul is untouchable by any apparent condition of earthly life. Thus you are free of all disease and assured of the life that spans eternity.

The Only Way To Heal

There is but one way to heal:
See only perfection.

The Kingdom that you seek
is found only by seeing all of life
through the eyes of innocence.

Do not complicate perfection
with concepts of healing.
All power of Heaven and earth
is given to those
who see Life as it is.

Healing
Begins In Your Mind

All healing begins in your mind.

Think positively,
see the good in all persons
and circumstances,
and remember
that God is always present.

Invite the Holy Spirit
into your life
and expect only the best
in all your activities.

As your soul is healed,
your body will become new.
The door to peace
is opened with your mind,
and the Kingdom
entered through your heart.

The Christ

The Christ is not a person, but a Force. It is the energy of true healing, the direct expression to God and route Home to Him.

The Christ will empower you in your healing. Those who truly heal must acknowledge the presence of Christ in all service. This is how you align yourself with the energy to accomplish all, and let it be done instantaneously. You are a channel for the healing light, a living vessel for the birth of love on the planet earth.

Jesus was rightly called the Christ because he was completely identified with the Force of Love that flowed to this world through him. He was one man who knew his true identity as a Son of God.

Now this man, this Jesus, this Christ, calls to you to share his identity. He reaches out in a call for saviors of the world, beckoning all who would invoke the Christ power in the healing of the planet and all who share life with it. His hand is extended to you, inviting you to join the force of all men and women who will bear witness to the truth of our perfect light.

The Christ is looking for healers. Would you be one of them? If so, simply acknowledge His Presence. Thus you are heir to all the blessings that bring healing to all who seek it.

The Call To Heal

You are called by the Christ to heal your brethren and the earth. Do not underestimate the urgency of this responsibility or your ability to fulfill it. All of your experiences have prepared you for this role, which you have already undertaken.

Those who come to you for guidance are not sent by happenstance. The great Plan of Good for their lives is joined with yours. You meet by divine appointment.

With gratitude and encouragement, accept all who request your help, for their healing is yours. Be a light to all who sincerely seek to come out of the darkness into the light.

Call on the Father to serve humanity through you, and you, along with everyone you touch, will know the Peace of God.

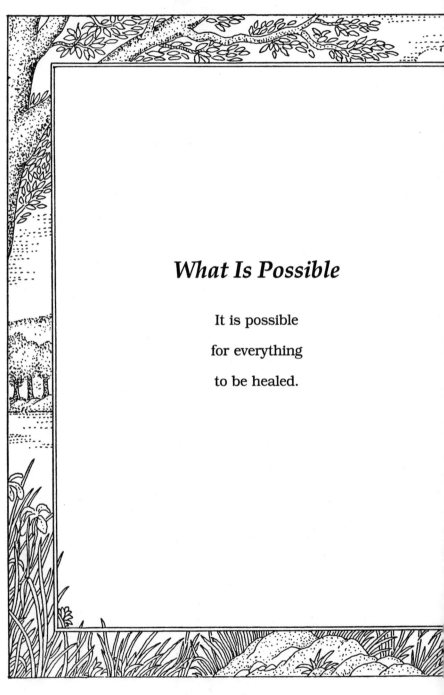

What Is Possible

It is possible

for everything

to be healed.

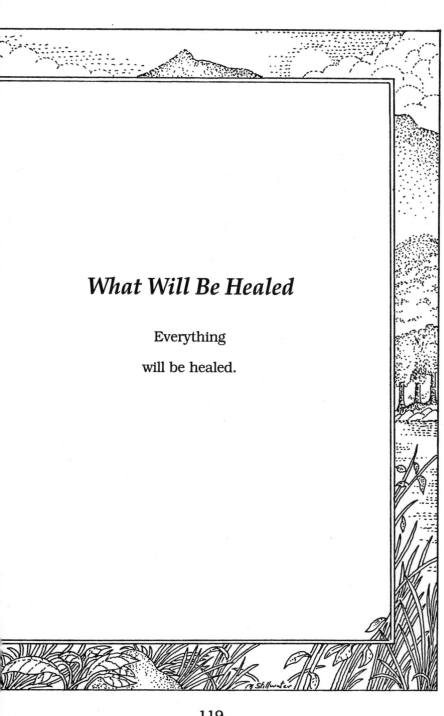

What Will Be Healed

Everything

will be healed.

The Beams
of Virtue

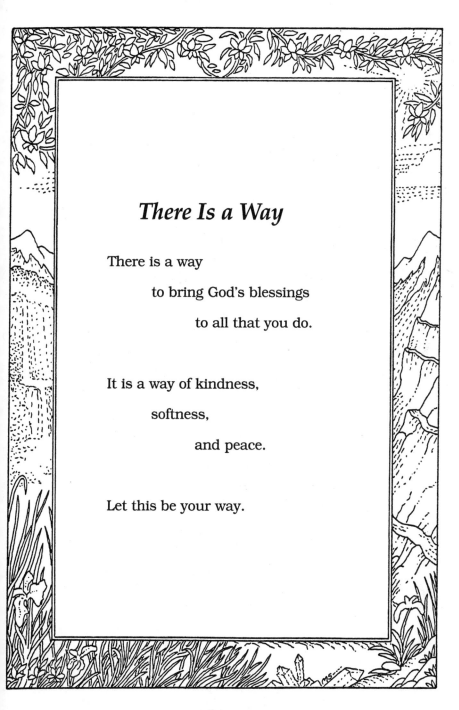

There Is a Way

There is a way

       to bring God's blessings

              to all that you do.

It is a way of kindness,

       softness,

              and peace.

Let this be your way.

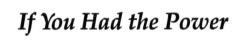

If You Had the Power

If you had the power
to heal the suffering of humanity,
would you do it?

If your love could relieve
the burden of the downcast,
would you give it?

If you were endowed with a light
that could bring peace
to everyone you meet,
would you shine it?

All of these gifts
are within your hands now.
Your brothers and sisters
are reaching out to you for love.

Now is your time
to be the light of the world,
for that is what you are.

The Time Has Come

The time has come for you to lay aside your worldly burdens and live for God alone. This has been your wish for so long, and now it is possible.

The playthings of your childhood are fallen away, and you can no longer delay living your purpose in the world.

Remember the vow you made in your heart of hearts long ago, at a time that your mortal mind cannot recall, but your soul remembers well.

Come, lay aside your worldly treasures that have brought you only hardship, and take my hand to walk with me in my Father's Kingdom, prepared for us since the world began. Together we will know the light that makes us one.

The Courage To Live For God

Have the courage to live for God.

Remember
that every kind word and deed
helps others
and changes the world.

Do not fear to stand for
your heart's faith.
Speak to your brother's soul,
and he will understand.

Even blind men can feel
what they cannot see.

Responsibility

Accept responsibility for your life,

and God will help you far more

than when you depended on Grace.

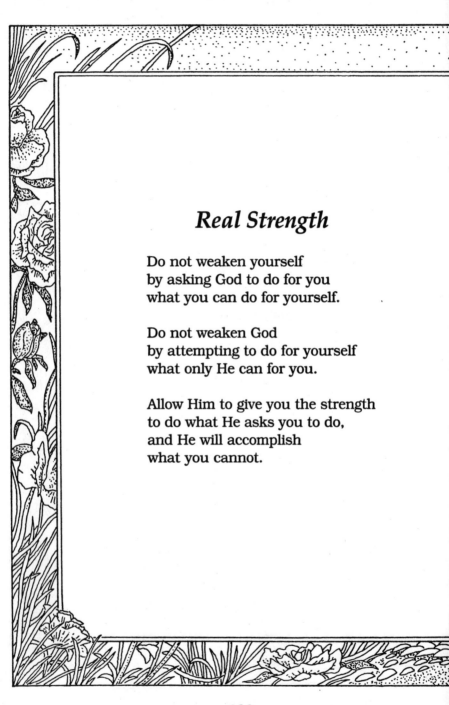

Real Strength

Do not weaken yourself
by asking God to do for you
what you can do for yourself.

Do not weaken God
by attempting to do for yourself
what only He can for you.

Allow Him to give you the strength
to do what He asks you to do,
and He will accomplish
what you cannot.

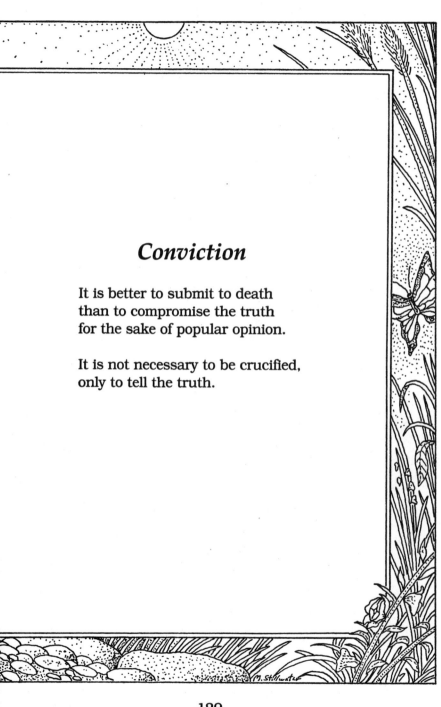

Conviction

It is better to submit to death
than to compromise the truth
for the sake of popular opinion.

It is not necessary to be crucified,
only to tell the truth.

The Saint and
The Worldly Man

The difference between the saint and the worldly man is this: The worldly man flees from problems, while the saint embraces them as opportunities to heal humanity.

When you overcome an obstacle through love, you participate in gaining grace for all of your brothers.

Do not underestimate the service you render when you conquer a personal challenge. When you rise above circumstances, you gain not only for yourself, but for every soul who must face the same trial.

There is no greater gift that you can offer to the whole of humanity than the mastery of your own life.

The Apostles

My apostles are those
who live my teaching.

I care not for name, form,
or outer show,
but for the intention of your actions.

Do not believe for a moment
that I have restricted my grace
to a chosen few of old.
You may follow in their footsteps,
if you like,
but go on to blaze a new path
of light and love
with your own hands and feet.

I will guide you.

Fully and Wholly

Make not a mockery of my teachings
by spewing them out of your mouth
like unswallowed food.
Even a parrot can be taught
to utter holy words.

You have the great
and glorious capacity
to step out of darkness
and walk in light.

You can give loving kindness
in a way that
no hypocrite can imitate.
You can become the Christ
fully and wholly.
Thus you are my apostle.

Anyone who continues my life,
I call my own.

Your Part Is Crucial

You have come into this life
for a very specific purpose.

Always remember
that you have an essential role
in the liberation
of all of your brothers and sisters.

Your every step will be illuminated.

Your Profession

From this moment on, you have a new profession: a minister of God to all the world. No longer are you a businessman, a teacher, or a doctor as you have been trained. Your business is sharing the light.

You are to teach only love. Everyone you meet, see, or think of is your patient, come to you for the healing of their spirit by your forgiveness. Make your office a temple of the Living Power of Love.

Everyone you touch will feel the hand of the Christ comforting him. Everyone who shares your presence will find support, encouragement, and new belief in himself.

Let your heart shine so purely that everyone who thinks of you remembers God. They will leave you uplifted, renewed, and reborn.

Be an inspiration to all the world, and all the world will be an inspiration to you.

Your Song

Your song is the healer of the world.

Every note of love you sing
in the melody of your life
is the keynote on which
a host of angelic light is born
to bless all the cosmos
with the gift of harmony.

As you walk the world
sharing your song,
I will fill your cup
with the nectar of joy
that will stir all who hear
your melody
to remember theirs.

Divine Possibilities

As a minister of God
you do not need to stop
what you are doing.

Simply reorder your priorities.

Your actions are opportunities
for God to bless the world
through you.

The Hand of the Divine
is in every encounter.
Your adventure is to discover
the divine possibilities in yourself
and everyone you meet.

When you walk with God,
your days are filled with joy.

Be a Channel

God is using you
as a messenger of peace.

The channels are open for you
to hear His gentle bidding.

Your direction is given you now.

God will do all through you.

Quiet Time

Give yourself quiet time
to listen to the soothing voice
of your Heavenly Father.
He will speak to you.

You live in a busy world.
You have duties to perform
and responsibilities to enact.
You can find a few moments
to allow the light to fill you.

God does not want you to run
from the world.
Quite the contrary;
He wants you to shine His love
into life
from within life.

To live for God,
you must allow Him to live in you.

The quiet time that you give to Spirit
will bear fruit a thousand times over.

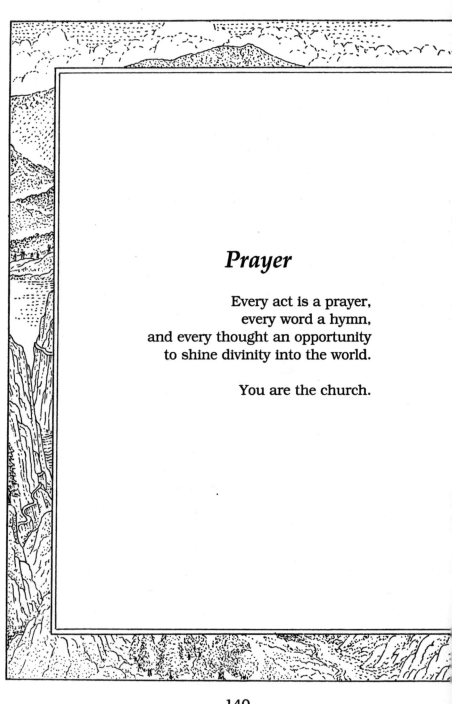

Prayer

Every act is a prayer,
every word a hymn,
and every thought an opportunity
to shine divinity into the world.

You are the church.

The Most
Powerful Prayer

The most powerful prayer is
"Thank you."

Instead of asking God
for what you want,
thank Him for what you have.
Then you will realize
that you already have
all you could possibly want.

Thanksgiving satisfies the heart
in a way that supplication cannot.

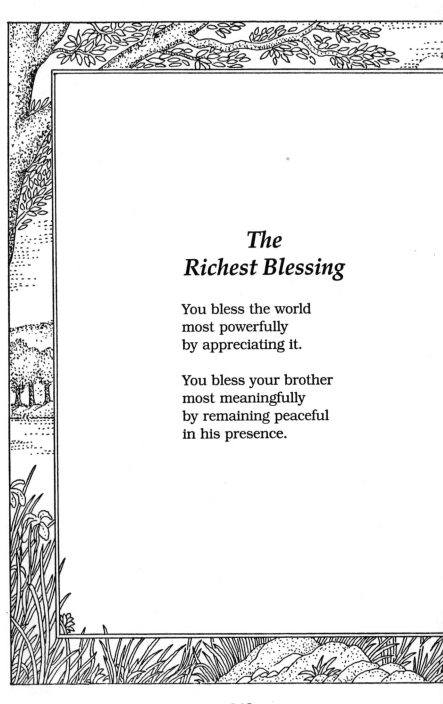

The
Richest Blessing

You bless the world
most powerfully
by appreciating it.

You bless your brother
most meaningfully
by remaining peaceful
in his presence.

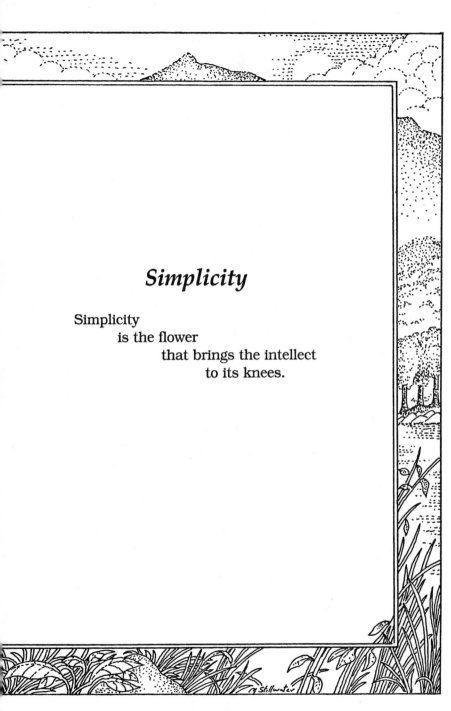

Simplicity

Simplicity
      is the flower
           that brings the intellect
           to its knees.

Gentleness

You give your brethren healing through your gentle touch. It is within your power to offer a soothing balm to heal the wounds of their spirit.

Never underestimate the healing power of a soft and kindly touch. Your hands are the hands of Christ. They are gifts through which you can lift away the suffering of the world.

When you touch another, let a sweet flow of healing love pass between you. Be a channel for the Force that is given you from above. As you are willing to receive God's power, it flows through you for the benefit of all.

Be gentle, be strong, and be willing to share. As you give the blessing of a healing touch, you receive it.

God's gifts are freely given.

Wonder

Walk in a continuous
state of wonder.
The holiest angels
live in constant celebration.

You may gauge
your spiritual growth
by the expansion
of your sense
of the miraculous.

Everything that happens to you
is a miracle
because *you* are a miracle.

Modesty

Be modest.
Your strength lies in balance.

Moderation is a noble trait
which the world overlooks.

Be a student of the middle way,
and your walk will be
steady and sure.

You will reach peace
by way of peace.

Words

Words are cups.
Their worth depends upon
the spirit invested in them.

When you speak,
imbue your words with divine love
and healing power.
Let them be a blessing
to your brethren.

In this way you are an emissary
of Divine Light.

Ceremony

Ceremony is a vehicle to know God.

Performed with love,
ceremony links your mind
with the Power that created you.

Struggled through as a drudgery,
ceremony has ceased to serve
its function
and is better left undone.

You cannot come to God
by obligation.
The heart is obliged
only to love.

Let your whole life
be a celebration of the heart.

Work

Work happily.

Make all of your deeds

an offering of joy,

and work will become play.

The amount that you do

is not as important

as the attitude

with which you do it.

Success

Allow the Holy Spirit

to work through you,

and everything you do

will be successful.

In God there is no failure.

Holiness

Holiness is not the result
of an act that you do.
It is the contentment you enjoy
when you live in harmony
with your true being.

Seek not to attain holiness
through righteous actions,
but let the divinity of your nature
emanate from you
because God created you
in wisdom.

There is One within you
who eternally remembers
your preciousness.

Remember it with Him.

Giving

Whenever you give to one person,
you are giving to all.
Whatever you give to a brother
you are giving to yourself.

There is no slight act
of thoughtfulness;
every act of kindness
is supremely powerful.

Money

Money is your friend because it is your mirror. Because money is nothing, it allows you to see what you believe about yourself, your brothers, your life, and God.

Use money as holy, and you bless the world. Make it evil, and you curse yourself.

The purpose of money is to help you learn the healing power of giving and receiving blessing.

The Holy Spirit has a purpose for everything, far more wonderful than the limited purposes the world has assigned. Money will teach you that the gold within you far outshines the currency you handle.

Food

Do not make food your god.

Make God your food.

One Life to Live

While your lives may be many,

this is the life to which

you must devote yourself

wholeheartedly.

The opportunities

before you now

are extremely valuable.

You will gain for all

by using them wisely.

All Power

You give power
to that which you are against.

Be against nothing,
and all power remains within you,
where it was given to be.

To be against anything
is to dream of a will alien to God's.
Do not give reality to the illusion
that there could be something
outside of Him.

Hate not evil;
only love the Truth.
Be not against anything;
be only for love.

All evil vanishes
from the life of one
who keeps love in his heart.

The Secret of Mastery

What comes of itself, let it come. What goes of itself, let it go. This is the secret of mastery of life.

Real peace lies in offering all circumstances and decisions to the One who sees their blessing. Find comfort in God's perfect presence.

Do not force your will upon another. Simply listen for the way Spirit would have you follow. Follow the cues and you will find that the flexible is stronger than the resistant. There is no resistance in God.

Grasp this simple formula for abundant living, and you will find only ease, for you will recognize the good in all.

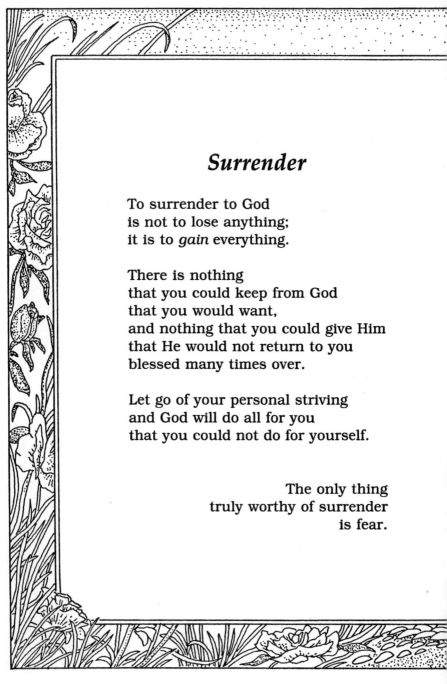

Surrender

To surrender to God
is not to lose anything;
it is to *gain* everything.

There is nothing
that you could keep from God
that you would want,
and nothing that you could give Him
that He would not return to you
blessed many times over.

Let go of your personal striving
and God will do all for you
that you could not do for yourself.

> The only thing
> truly worthy of surrender
> is fear.

The Corpses

The corpses to mourn for
are not those buried in the earth.
The people you lament are not there.

Only the dead bury the dead,
and only the dead
feel lost in their absence.

The corpses to pray for
are the living dead,
who walk among you
with troubled visage
and decaying demeanor.

None are so lamentable
as the living dead,
and no souls
are more worthy of your prayer.

Be sure you are not among them.

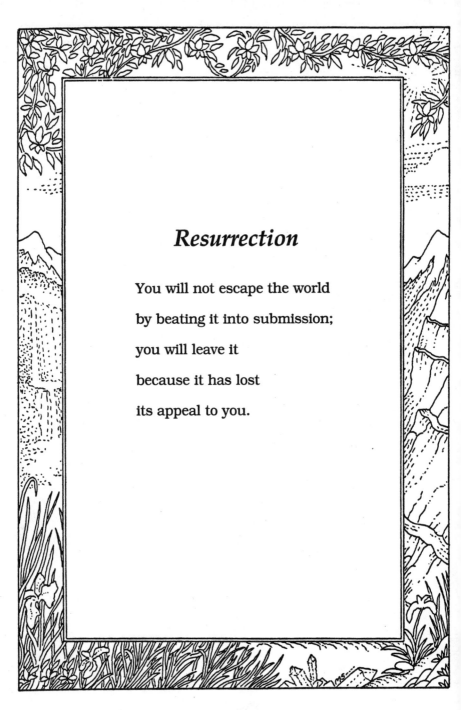

Resurrection

You will not escape the world

by beating it into submission;

you will leave it

because it has lost

its appeal to you.

The
Crest Jewels
of
Illumination

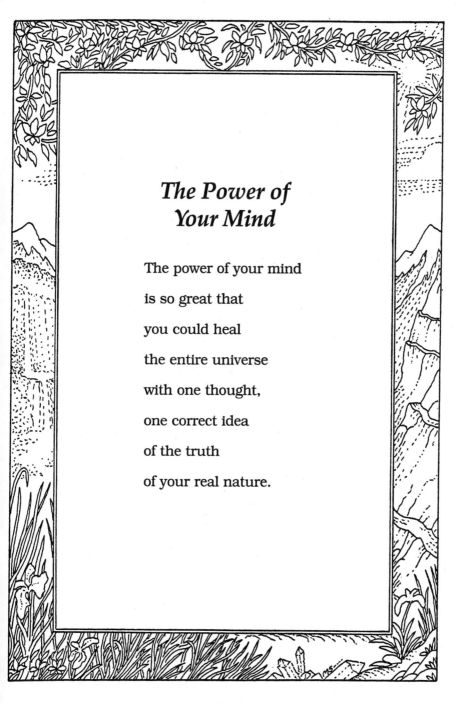

The Power of Your Mind

The power of your mind

is so great that

you could heal

the entire universe

with one thought,

one correct idea

of the truth

of your real nature.

Choice and Destiny

Choice is what you made

when you committed yourself

to live for God.

Now it is your destiny.

Mind and Heart

The mind thinks,
while the heart knows.
The purpose of your mind
is to think true thoughts,
and the purpose of your heart
is to know true love.

The marriage of a pure mind
and a loving heart
offers peace and strength
that reflect
the dignity of Heaven.
Live with the integrity
of loving and being,
and you are whole.

Truth and Appearances

Do not pay attention
to appearances
which guide you
to the fiction of separation
instead of the truth of unity.

No one who knows the truth
could submit to
false instruction.

Flesh and Spirit

The answer to your problems
lies not in changing
what you do;
it is in changing
the way you think
about what you do.

Change your thoughts
and you will be reborn.
What is born of flesh is flesh;
what is born of Spirit is Spirit.

Heaven and Hell

Love is Heaven,
and fear is hell.

Do not wait
for Heaven or hell
in an afterlife.
There is no afterlife;
there is only life.

Heaven and hell
are available to you now,
depending on your choice
for love or fear.
Choose Heaven now,
and you need never
fear hell again.

Loss and Gain

Loss is impossible.

See your losses as gains,

and you will laugh

at the notion of lack.

You have always had

everything you need,

and always will.

No Sacrifice

Sacrifice is not necessary,
because it is impossible.

You cannot lose
what you never had,
but you can gain
what you have always had.

The Kingdom has been
held in store for you
at no cost whatsoever.

No Mystery

There are no mysteries
in Heaven.
All in God's world is fresh,
clean, and shining
for everyone to see
and know clearly.
God has nothing to hide,
and because you are one
with Him,
neither do you.

The truth is always obvious
unless you cover it with fear.
Your Father has made it
the simplest of all tasks
to be aware of who He is,
because His greatest joy
is in your discovery
of who you are.

The truth welcomes all who
would believe in it.

The Unreality
of Sin

Sin does not exist
in the mind of God.

Evil is the creation
of fearful thoughts;
therefore it has never been.

Let your mind
be the Mind of God,
and sin departs
from your consciousness
forever.

The Healing
of Guilt

Guilt can never be

eradicated by action,

only healed by love.

Awakening

Replace every "evil"
in the Bible
with "unconsciousness,"
and you will see
that all you need to do
is awaken.

Replace "devil"
with "fear,"
and you will see
there is nothing to give
but love.

Replace "God" and "Christ"
with "My Divine Self"
and you will see that
the Bible was written
by you,
about you,
and for you.

What to Value

Value only what has
no beginning or end.

When you know
what is given to you
by your Father,
you bring Heaven to earth.

What to Pray For

Do not pray
for events,
circumstances,
or things.

Pray for the Peace of God.

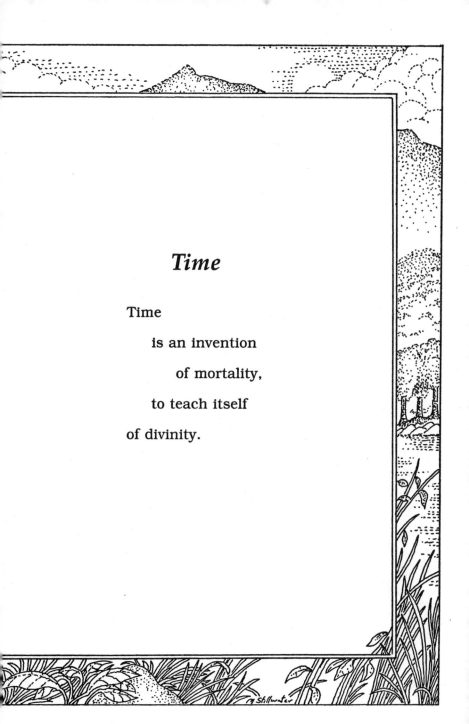

Time

Time

    is an invention

        of mortality,

    to teach itself

of divinity.

The Time of Salvation

Salvation has no future tense.
To be saved,
you must *be* saved.

All of your plans for salvation
must fail,
and blessedly so,
for a plan for salvation
denies the reality
of salvation now.
Thank God that
your plan must fail, and
His must succeed.

If you do not believe
you are already saved,
you never will be.

If you know you are saved,
you realize that
you always have been.

Salvation's Ease

Salvation is much easier

than you thought it to be,

for God's way is always easier

than the ego's.

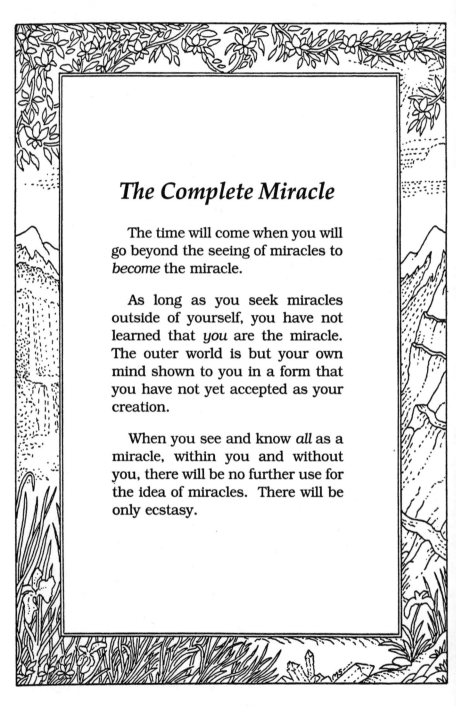

The Complete Miracle

The time will come when you will go beyond the seeing of miracles to *become* the miracle.

As long as you seek miracles outside of yourself, you have not learned that *you* are the miracle. The outer world is but your own mind shown to you in a form that you have not yet accepted as your creation.

When you see and know *all* as a miracle, within you and without you, there will be no further use for the idea of miracles. There will be only ecstasy.

Fear Not in the Valley

God is Only Love

In a time of shadows
you need only remind yourself,
"God is love, and only love.
If I am seeing something
other than love,
I must be seeing something that
is not really there."

Dear one,
you need no advice but this
to carry you all the way home
to the arms of the One
who knows only
your perfection.

Where Love Abides

I do not know evil,
therefore thoughts of evil
have no power over me.

Fear cannot enter
into my Kingdom,
for my Kingdom
is that of my Father,
where only love abides.

Fortitude

Your times of challenge are your greatest opportunities for spiritual advancement. When you find the peaceful solution to your uneasiness, you grow into your own strength.

See your challenges as gifts, for they are the keys to your healing and spiritual awakening. Every difficulty will vanish in the face of love and sincerity.

When confronted with a problem, ask yourself, "What solution will bring the peace of God to all concerned?" There is always a solution that will satisfy the soul. Patiently listen to the answer that heals, and act upon it with confidence.

God has no problems, only solutions.

Confidence

Have confidence that God
is working through you.

No matter what errors
you have made,
believe that your efforts
are being directed by God.

Continuously express
the highest good you can see,
and consecrate your acts
for the service of all.

When you believe in yourself,
you affirm God.

Only Life

All that you see of death
is your fear of it.
If you were to look truly
upon death,
you would see
the nothingness that it is.
You need not be concerned
in the least about death,
because it does not exist.

Learn that only life is real,
and live in freedom.
Recognize death
as nothing more
than an illusion of fear,
and walk in the dignity of life.

The universe is founded in life.
There are no exceptions to joy.

The Impossibility of Death

Death exists only in the past, the future, and the mortal mind, and therefore it does not exist at all. Live in the holy instant, and you will never know death.

Your Heavenly Father does not know death because He did not make it. Affirm what He knows, and live in eternal glory. Deny what He does not recognize, and you are free.

The Answer to Satan

Here is the final solution
to all of your questions and
problems about satan:
Satan is nothing more than
the sense of separation
that seems to make
boundaries between brothers.

Satan has no force,
no power,
and no will
but that which you give it
by your belief.

There is no force in the
universe outside of God.

No Need to Suffer

You do not need pain.

You do not need
to resist pain.

All that you need,
you already are.

The End of Pain

Pain comes
only of resistance.
Stop fighting,
and you end pain.

It is possible
to live without pain.
Experiment with this truth,
and it will prove itself to you.

The End of Suffering

The end of suffering
will not come with an action,
but with an awareness.

The moment you realize
that your Heavenly Father
takes no joy in your suffering,
neither will you.

Thus is your healing
accomplished,
along with
the entire family of God.

Perfect Light

Fear is ignorance.
There is no reason
to fear anything.
Love,
and fear disappears
like a nightmare.

The day will come
when all fear
shall depart
from your heart,
and you will live
in perfect light.

M. Stillwater

The
Golden
Destiny

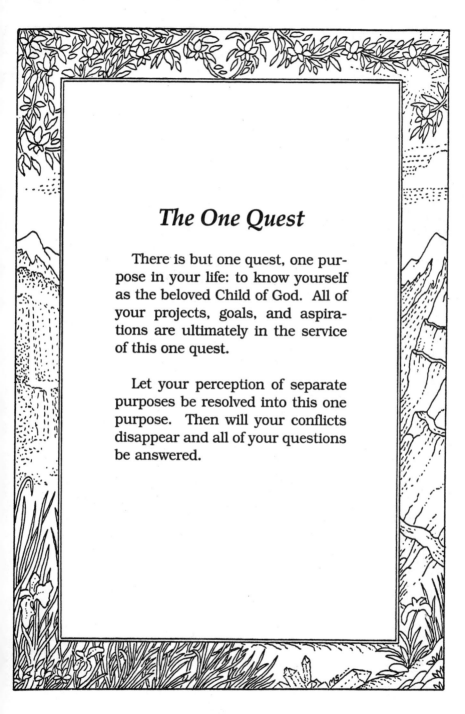

The One Quest

There is but one quest, one purpose in your life: to know yourself as the beloved Child of God. All of your projects, goals, and aspirations are ultimately in the service of this one quest.

Let your perception of separate purposes be resolved into this one purpose. Then will your conflicts disappear and all of your questions be answered.

The Wondrous Journey

Your life has not been a vain wandering, but a wonderful and marvelous journey toward the Divine light which your soul has always remembered, even while your conscious mind has been unaware.

For aeons have you searched and wandered through the plains of earthly questing, steadily, surely, being prodded to the reawakening of your soul's purpose.

All of your seeking, striving, and learning has led you to this point. Claim the Golden Kingdom as your own, and uplift your brethren into the glories that await them. The riches of Heaven belong to you.

Your Limits

Your limits
are nothing more
than your idea of
what you have already done.

They have nothing to do
with what you can
and will do.

Your Future

Your future will not be
anything like your past.

The complete release
of your past,
gently given to God
to replace it with a
perfect destiny,
is the requirement
for your entry
to the Kingdom.

The New Life

There is a new life
in store for you,
one marked by its simplicity.

You veered from your heritage
when you agreed
on complicated concepts.

Words may lead you
to the gate of your home,
but silence
takes you through the door.

Now is the Time

Sisters and Brothers of Light, now is your time for action. All of your incarnations, all of your history, and all of your dreams are culminated in this moment. You stand at the threshold of the answers to your prayers. Why tarry at the door?

All that you do at this time is of crucial importance. You have been entrusted with the power to mark the destiny of all living things. Never underestimate your power to create positive change. It is man who has wrought all of the difficulties in the world, and only man who can remove them.

This is the promise in your hour of trial: Everyone on earth will enter the Kingdom of Heaven and transform the earth into the expression of God.

All for Now

All of the work
done by all of the saints
has been directed
to this moment,
to you.

You are charged with
the responsibility to deliver
the accumulated blessings
of your spiritual forebears
to humanity.

This task is not beyond
your capacity.
It is your only purpose.

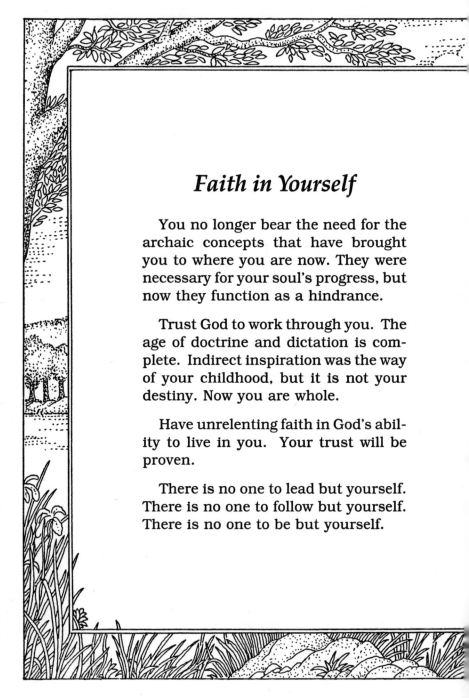

Faith in Yourself

You no longer bear the need for the archaic concepts that have brought you to where you are now. They were necessary for your soul's progress, but now they function as a hindrance.

Trust God to work through you. The age of doctrine and dictation is complete. Indirect inspiration was the way of your childhood, but it is not your destiny. Now you are whole.

Have unrelenting faith in God's ability to live in you. Your trust will be proven.

There is no one to lead but yourself. There is no one to follow but yourself. There is no one to be but yourself.

Your Dream

There is no power in the universe that can stand between you and your dream.

No matter what empty fantasies you have indulged, you have one dream that must be fulfilled: your awakening to your own perfection.

Until that dream is more real than your passing fantasies, your aspiration will guide you like a guiding star in a dark night, continually, eternally calling you to claim the light that is your self.

With the morning comes awakening. The truth of day shines the night away entirely.

Your Inheritance

Your inheritance
must be peace,
for that is
your Father's nature.

You are destined
to inherit
the entire Kingdom.

Gifts

Gifts are being given you now in great measure. Appreciate them as such, and be the bearer of glad tidings to all you meet.

You are embarked upon a great and glorious adventure — the unfoldment of the flower of your destiny, a process that has been quickening over the centuries and is now ready to bear the sweetest fruit within your soul.

Hasten to live for the light, and be a lamp unto the world.

Religion

The ego has misused religion as it has distorted every ray of truth shined upon a darkened world. It has taken a beam of unity and perverted it to create separation and fear.

Every religion was born on a wave of wonder given to guide the family of humankind home to its source, and every religion has been used by unconsciousness to pirate this sacred journey for twisted purposes.

The time for the reunion of all religions is come. No more must you use the Truth to justify falsehood. No more must you put a limitation on light. No more must you assign superiority as a substitute for oneness.

Your function at this time is to find the Truth that identifies all religions as one. Hold your lamp very high that all people may see that God is true in all forms.

Here is the test by which you may prove the truth of a pathway: Does it include the entire family of humankind as divine? Does it place forgiveness above judgment? Does it honor God's willingness to speak to and redeem every soul? And yea, here is the ultimate proof: Does it bring the Peace of God to all who follow its course?

These are the signals of the true religion, the hallmarks of the New Age. Honor all who have brought the Light of God into the world, for all the saints of all the religions have had but one cause: the fulfillment of love on the planet earth, surely accomplished by celebrating the unity of all people and all life.

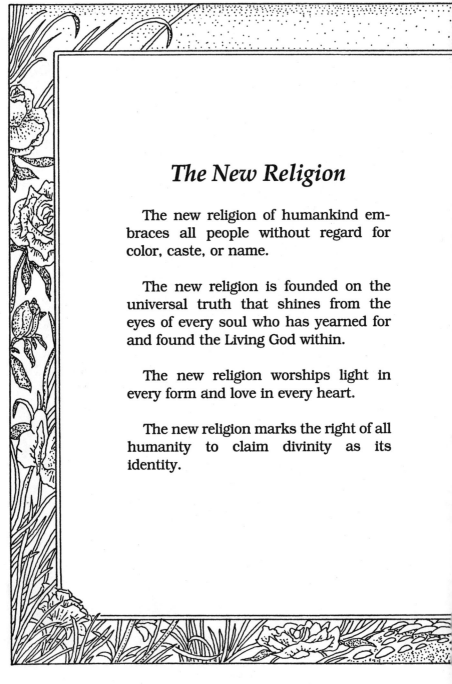

The New Religion

The new religion of humankind embraces all people without regard for color, caste, or name.

The new religion is founded on the universal truth that shines from the eyes of every soul who has yearned for and found the Living God within.

The new religion worships light in every form and love in every heart.

The new religion marks the right of all humanity to claim divinity as its identity.

The Time of Unity

The time of separation of religions, races, and pathways is now come to an end.

All of these forms were necessary to develop certain wisdom in the family of humanity, but now their usefulness has been accomplished.

There is no difference in the God that the religions worship, and so there is no difference in the religions.

You are entering an age in which the oneness of all things is glorified. All of history has led to this point, and blessed are you who behold its reality.

The Wonder

The New Age is more glorious than any concept you have thought it to be. To know the wonder in store for you, you must know the glory within you.

Become as little children – let your imagination soar beyond itself and fly you to a world where the bounty of your hope exceeds all the miracles you have awaited. Come to a land where innocence, goodness, and ease celebrate the joys of the heart. Enter the realm of being and knowing, rejoicing, and thanksgiving.

There is only good. There is only God. There is only love.

The New Age

The New Age is far beyond time. The New Age is a consciousness into which you may freely enter at any moment you choose.

The New Age is the Garden of Eden, the Millennium, and Heaven, made complete as one.

You stand now at the threshold of the New Age, which honors the sanctity of all life as it celebrates the reality of God.

The New Age is now.

Your Goal

There is one goal that will never fail
you, a purpose which will heal your
mind the moment you realize its power.
Every goal in the world must bow to
your goal of true love.

When the happiness of your brethren
becomes your own, all of your questions
will fly away like dark birds of woe
scattering at the sound of laughter.
What separate interests could stand
before the golden ideal of harmony on
the earth?

Seek peace, not only for yourself, but for all the shining ones who share destiny's pathway with you. Then you will find a fulfillment beyond your highest expectations.

Seek love for all, and the joy that comes to all will be your own.

Seek a joined purpose, and every conflict will melt before the sun of shared understanding.

There is no power in the universe that can challenge the miracle of a loving heart. This is your goal, and you are destined to live it.

The Kingdom is Ready

Your preparation
for the work is complete.
It is the folly of earth to prepare
for the world to come.
The world to come *has* come,
and it lives within you now.

Be calm, be aware,
and be steadfast.
The Kingdom is ready.

Awaken and live in your
Father's House.

Peace on Earth

Peace on earth is possible.

Your belief in its possibility
is the seed.

Plant the seed,
and God will nurture it.

Then you can harvest
and enjoy it with God.

M.Stillwater